Memories of a Kentish Village, a
childhood spent in more innocent times

By John F Bennett
Foreword by Sir Michael Morpurgo OBE
Illustrations by Jessica Hayes

Authors note

This book depicts life in a quiet rural village in Kent, it represents the story of thousands of people of my generation who enjoyed a simple upbringing, we were all different but essentially the same. The children from the war generation with the memories of their parents still fresh from harder times.

Introduction

I was born in the hamlet of Bramling, part of the parish of Ickham and Well, located to the South East of the city of Canterbury. It is in this area where I grew up and spent most of my formative years.

I have been asked on numerous occasions to write my story, but was always unsure who would actually want to read my memories.

My father was Fred Bennett, local shopkeeper, historian and supporter of the villages where he was born, grew up and lived most of his life until retirement in 1991. He then moved a mile down the road to a quiet bungalow with my mother Gladys, in the village of Littlebourne.

I decided to write this book before fact became just hearsay. For years my ad was regarded as the font of knowledge for all things Ickham, Wickhambreaux and Bramling and all things local.

Of course, the local village knowledge guru Len Coombs, organist in the parish churches, shopkeeper and former teacher at the Simon Langton boys' school in Canterbury, was the 'go to' person before him and the many who passed before them, had carried the torch.

Len wrote an interesting and factual book about Ickham in 1976 which I have used as a cross checker to my memories. Dad did try and write some stories down and dictate a few stories on a Dictaphone, but he could not get to grips with the way it worked.

He was interviewed by one of the local university researchers about his extensive knowledge on the pill boxes around the area. He of course as a young teenager would have 'supervised' the building of each one personally as is the way of children!

Dad's accounts of his childhood during the early years of World War two are in the care of the village, currently residing with Ickham resident Alan Jones. If someday we have a rural life museum set up in the area these, I am sure, will feature prominently.

Living and growing up in the 60s and 70s was probably one of the best times in living memory, a sense of austerity still permeated through daily life, but the changes in technology that were fast approaching, had not yet arrived with the force that drives our everyday lives.

Things were still simple and as such, we were a simple group of children untouched by sometimes the harsh realities of life. Dad always felt he had a story to tell but didn't quite know how to go about it.

I had a high-pressure job working away from home during the week so I was unable to help him achieve his desire.

I have now recorded my memories in the chapters to follow, from the earliest memories through to a wild teenager with a moped!

The memories contained in this publication, together with some of the background information, will aid newcomers to the area, and those with a sense of village history, to get the feel of life in a village, which all those before have contributed to in no small measure. I am not a writer, just a person who recognises the importance of recording history as accurately as possible.

I record incidents as I remember them but are careful not to mention names where possible, unless critical to the story we all contributed, this is the story of our generation.

If through the passage of time I have made mistakes and events or places are incorrect, then I am happy for changes to be made on future editions.

Foreword.

It is rare to come across a book where the reader can share so many vivid memories with the author. By happenstance I spent my last years as a schoolteacher living just outside a small village called Wickhambreaux.

I taught in the village school there for a while. and it was in the mobile classroom there, teaching 10 and 11year olds, that I began to find my voice as a storyteller, by reading and telling stories to the children. This, it turns out, is John's own country. Only he knows it a lot better than I do.

My own children went to Wickhambreaux school, began their education there. I coached the school football team, with not much success, but we had fun. Our worst defeat was against Littlebourne. Score, Littlebourne 10 Wickhambreaux 0.

I helped produce the Nativity play at Christmas, which was less disastrous, and also great fun. I came to work on a moped, singing my way happily from our house down on the marshes near Stodmarsh. I had colleagues who became friends, and an inspiring Headteacher, Mrs Skiffington, who ran a happy school.

I looked forward to every day and that was mostly because of the children. They put up with me with good grace. We learnt together, all of us learning to grow up, to find our confidence and our voices, all of us discovering more about ourselves and each other and about the world about us. They were good days, memorable days.

But time can dim memories. Reading John's book brought back to us so vividly the place and the people. His book is filled with names familiar to us, but almost forgotten. He reminded us of how it was to live there, the lives of the children I taught. Like all good writers, he takes you by the hand and leads you into his story, the story of his childhood roaming far and wide in the villages and the marshes. His story echoed our story.

He writes in his book of playing as a boy in a wartime pillbox that I knew so well, where I knew the children played when we lived there. It was a secret den to them, a hideaway, a cave, a camp, a castle. It was any place they wanted it to be.

For me the pillbox became the place in which I set my very first published story, in 1974 I think, a story I first told to children in my mobile classroom at Wickhambreaux School, the story Mrs Skiffington encouraged me to send off to a publisher. I called the book, It Never Rained. It's a collection of five short stories set in and around exactly the same part of the world that John describes so well in his book. In it there is a story called The Castle in the Field.

But why is it important to tell such stories, fiction like mine, or nonfiction like John's? Because history matters. We should know how people lived, who lived where. Thomas Hardy called it 'the old association'. We need to know and understand the lives of those who came before us, who built this house, who last milled corn in the mill by the stream, who lived in this house on the green, who planted that chestnut tree. That way a place comes alive for us, through the people who made it. John and I both are passing on our stories, each in his own voice, in his own way.

As you read this book, live it in your mind's eye with John. It's a wonderful voyage of discovery. It's the Cider with Rosie or the Lark Rise to Candleford of East Kent. Enjoy it.

Michael Morpurgo.

Dedicated to the memory of my father, Fred Bennett and villagers who live, and who have lived in the parishes of Ickham & Well and Wickhambreaux.

Chapter one. The early years

I was born into a rural working-class family in 1957 with most of my grandparents, uncles, aunts and cousins living within an easy walk. We lived in White cottage in Bramling, right on the main road, the A257.

In the early 1960s this was a very quiet road and traffic was almost non-existent. Being born twelve years after the end of World War 2, the adult conversation and anecdotes were mainly from that period.

This of course for most people of that generation, was the most exciting period of their lives. With the fear and uncertainty of not knowing how the war was affecting them or relatives away in far flung parts of the world.

The parents and grandparents of this era had gone through this upheaval sometimes twice within living memory. Unlike the world of today, when the internet brings us up to date and live information on world events is plastered across the television as it happens.

The only information available back then was seemingly censored newspapers, carefully scripted and conservative information released in broadcasts, for the few people who owned a new-fangled radio.

Music during this era was primarily 1940s big band music my parents enjoyed during their earlier years, interspersed with the 1950s romantic ballads by the likes of Doris Day and Guy Mitchell. Rock and Roll had not permeated into our household.

The preparation for Sunday lunch times was always to the tunes of *'Three Way Family Favourites'* on the Light program on the BBC broadcast simultaneously from London, Germany and Hong Kong with Cliff Michelmore and his wife Jean Metcalf. The household interest in all thing's military was abound with constant reminiscence.

When I was just a few weeks old, I was in my cot in the corner of the lounge fast asleep with the pet Labrador dozing next to me. Mum went to the kitchen and almost instantly there was a huge crash, dust filled the air throughout the house.

When mum came back most of the lounge floor was missing and there I was, still asleep in my cot on the floor of the cellar with a confused black Labrador a lighter shade of grey!

My memories of my grandparents are quite vivid, my father's parents were quite different to my mother's, Grandad Bennett was a softly spoken man with a broad Kentish dialect, almost unheard nowadays, who worked for HW Mount on a fruit farm in Littlebourne.

After he retired from the farm, he became the village postman for many years until ill health and advancing years, curtailed his ability to work.

Nanny Bennett looked after my father's disabled sister who went everywhere with her as if she was her shadow. Nan always looked tired and worn out but sheer determination drove her out of bed every morning.

They lived in Ickham in one of the new post war council houses in Treasury View. Grandad was a keen gardener and always had a productive vegetable garden. My mother's parents were different, their home was full of chipped furniture, damaged ornaments and mismatched cutlery due to the bomb damage which they sustained while living in Folkestone.

Grandad Garrett was a quiet withdrawn man who sat in his chair by the fire but whenever I visited, he would often stare at me and sometimes appear to cry before walking out of the room.

He was prone to playing the old upright piano with some dexterity given the arthritis in his joints. He would play the World War One classics with gusto, but on closer inspection the tears would be running down his face. We could hear the sound of the piano across the road in our sitting room.

He looked so sad all the time. I don't remember him working, but he had hit retirement age when I was very young. He was suffering from what we now know as Post Traumatic Stress Disorder, from his experiences in the trenches during WW1.

This was compounded by the loss of his eldest son during the battle of Crete in 1941. This had a profound effect on him but this of course was lost on me as a four-year-old.

Nanny Garrett was a bright cheerful lady, a little wizened in her senior years but lively and full of fun. I spent quite a bit of time with her when I was a small child when my parents were working. I learnt some of the most bizarre things in life with my grandparents. Not many people of today's generation would know what a 'poke' was.

I was often asked to take the peelings and kitchen waste to the poke at the top of the garden. This was a deep hole on the ground, food waste was put in daily and when it was full, another would be dug out and the process repeated.

The original poke would be dug out about a year later at planting time and the composted remains would be spread around the garden as fertiliser. One of the local sayings was 'happy as a pig in a poke'.

I think this refers to an incident when a pig escaped its enclosure and came upon the poke as it made an escape from its inevitable fate.

Apparently, the pig was retrieved after being found face down in the poke eating as fast it could! During WW2 you could own and fatten a pig for the table but they had to be registered with the Ministry of Food.

At the back of the gardens behind the grandparent's houses were a line of small wooden sheds, these were very old and the timber showed evidence of disrepair. The roof or lack of it made the visit a quick affair.

These were the only toilets available to the houses. In my early days, the 'box' contained a chemical style toilet with a wedge of cut newspaper neatly threaded on a string!

To empty these was like a military operation, there was nowhere to empty this crude but essential devices. The neighbours used to creep out late at night, remove the bucket and climb over the low fence into the field, emptying the contents into a quickly dug hole along the fence line, on the farmers side of the field.

The smell of Jeyes fluid drifted across the gardens in the still summer air reminding everyone the toilets had just been emptied. When I smell Jeyes fluid today those memories make me smile and take me back to being four years old.

I imagine now this would have been fraught with dangers, spillage and contamination and choice language, would have provoked clothing removal before entering the house. The wash board would have had an early morning use the following day!

This must have been a step back in time for my grandparents, they had come from Folkestone during 1940, following a visit from an enemy bomb.

Flushing toilets and electric light would have been the norm there. Now gas lights were normal and toileting was as described as above!

My early years were spent in Bramling, only moving to Fern Cottage in Ickham when I was seven. Because the logistics of getting me to

Wickhambreaux school without a direct bus route, was impossible from there as my mother didn't drive at that time. I attended a school in Ash as the number thirteen bus stopped directly outside our house, and again right opposite the school.

It was named Wootenly House School now St Faith's, it was staffed by mainly ex-military teachers, who dressed the part, led by the headteacher, Miss Edna P Cowell, a formidable spinster who could bring a playground of screaming children to instant silence by just uttering a gentle cough. Such was the fear she instilled into youngsters of that time.

I remember vividly when I was four years old, I was put on the number 13 bus by my mother and made the trip to Ash all by myself! The panic only subsided when the bus stopped by the school and the driver said I could get off!

Some years later I asked why they chose to send me to the school which seemed so far away, the response was that as there were no other children in Bramling, getting me to school in Wickhambreaux or Wingham was too difficult for both working parents.

Wingham school was just a mile away but I didn't broach the subject? Maybe a bit of politics was in play? I didn't ask further!

The school in Ash was a private establishment, its fees were high even by today's standards. I don't know how my parents could afford them but later in life the answer presented itself.

My uncle Dennis had a good job working for the organisation later to be known as the Civil Aviation Authority, he was the equivalent of a director and obviously on a good salary. I believe he subsidised my primary education. I was very close to my uncle until he sadly passed away in the early 1980s.

I went to school with a diverse group of youngsters, there was the sons of two Lords, both now are sitting in the House of Lords, three who went on to be doctors, two vets, a couple of now retired senior Army officers and a plethora of barristers, solicitors and professionals in all fields and academia. I have a photograph somewhere and it looks like an edition of a junior who's who!

Because I had so much time off school, I found it difficult maintaining and developing friendships with my peer group, so there was a certain amount of isolation when at school.

It was decided that I should join the school orchestra, on the face of it, this sounded a good idea but most of its members were from wealthy families and had private lessons.

I did try to learn to try wind instruments but because of my weakened chest, I couldn't maintain the blowing for longer than a few moments. String instruments did fare a little better, but my brain couldn't get my hands to work independently.

One of the teachers suggested I try the triangle. This I was able to do but I am now convinced it was a just a way of engaging and focussing a difficult child!

I was duly issued a triangle and attended all the practice sessions. My input was minimal as the triangle was not a lead instrument, but it was a fantastic grounding of how the various instruments worked together, I was able to identify each of them just by hearing a few notes.

This inspired by love of classical music which has stayed with me for a lifetime. The time finally came when we had our first concert.

We worked closely with the Sydney Woodman school of dancing in Sandwich, where we held a joint event in the Guildhall in Sandwich. Our school's participation was tailored down with our repertoire reduced, due to the dance school paying for the venue! We played five pieces of music but the triangle was only involved in the last piece.

All the family came and sat there eagerly for my long-promised performance. They had to sit through loads of ballet and classical dance etc, until we came on at the very end. They must have been so bored as a bit of culture was not their thing at all!

I stood there in the middle, triangle poised, reading through the music and then finally on the final song my chance came, the final note of the concert was played by me 'ting', huge round of applause and a feeling of was that really worth it?

The 1980s song by the group Chicago, 'If you leave me now' has such a moment just after the introduction, there is a microscopic pause and then a solitary note played on a triangle with some force.

This makes me laugh every time I hear it even now it makes me collapse with laughter, and I am instantly taken back to that fateful concert!

Dad worked for the Coombs brothers in the village shop in Ickham. He had been there since leaving school, apart from three years in the RAF at the end of the war. I will share more information about the village shop a little further on.

The house in Bramling was basic and in need of modernisation, the only toilet was outside and needing emptying every few days, primitive by today's standards. I do recall having a 'gazunder', a large china pot with a handle under my bed so I didn't have to go outside in the middle of the night.

This together with the tin bath in front of the fire, formed so many of my early memories.

We didn't have electricity until just before we moved to Ickham. The routine of lighting gas lights every evening was done with care. I can remember the unique smell of the lamps as they warmed up lingering in the air for hours.

Entertainment in the evenings at home was very sedentary, the radio provided music, it was powered by a large battery, to a small child the words on the dial were memorised and visions of faraway places were explained. Hilversum, Oslo, Valencia, Brussels and Prague just a few that were scattered around the face plate.

My parents tried to explain where these exotic places were on a map, neither of them had visited them and could only speculate what delights these places held. These days they are a short aeroplane ride away and you could city hop all of them in a few days.

The radio was mostly set to 1500 metres on the long wave where the BBC Light program resided. The set was also able to receive short and medium wave transmissions but needed a special aerial.

Entertainment was limited to playing cards, reading or playing draughts, all in the low light of wall mounted gas lights. The smell of gas fumes and the gentle hiss of the gas jets formed a background which was oppressive, it was only when you went up to bed could you breathe fresh air.

One would these days wonder how you didn't get overcome by the poisonous fumes during these long evenings closed in, but the ill-fitting window sashes, and gaps under exterior doors provided a draught that just kept you alive, albeit with a headache.

Winter evenings were worse, they would go on for ever, after the six o'clock news, the evening meal would be cleared away and we would adjourn into the sitting room, the coal fire would have been lit in the hearth late afternoon and we would settle in for the evening.

As a child I would go to bed not long after this but I can imagine the adults staying up until 11pm listening to music and radio plays. This would have been the norm for all families before television came into their lives. Conversation about the day's events and reading would have filled the void before the day drew to a close.

Throughout the rest of the house, paraffin lamps and candles were the only form of lighting, a paraffin lamp on the landing was the only form of illumination upstairs, otherwise at night the house was in complete darkness.

There were candles at strategic places downstairs, kitchen, dining room, hall etc. they were used in favour of the gas lamps which obviously had a cost. The only heating was from the coal fire in the lounge.

Although we were right on the main road between Canterbury and Sandwich, the noise on the road was minimal, at night you could go an hour without hearing a vehicle on the road outside.

Absolute silence, something we just don't get today with the amount of traffic and the routine humdrum we have all around us.

To this day I have a fear of rats, I can't bear to see them it causes a shudder to go down my spine and I go cold at the thought of what they mean to me.

When I was about three years old, I recall waking in the night with one standing on my face looking straight at me, the memory is as vivid today as it was sixty odd years ago!

To put this into perspective, when I was serving in the Army, I had to disarm a gunman in

Kosovo just moments after he had shot someone and on balance, I am far more frightened of a rat! Such is the terror they hold for me.

One of the memories which is really anecdotal is the poor condition of the house we lived in. It was effectively a tied cottage belonging to Colonel Friend at Duckpitts farm. Mum had been his house keeper since 1940, gradually reducing the hours she worked as I became older.

The house in today's world would have been deemed uninhabitable, in the 1980s it was completely refurbished as great cost when the estate was sold off. I have recently seen the sales prospective and the building is completely unrecognisable to what I remember in 1962.

The only thing I remembered was the arches in the eaves on the third floor where it split into two rooms, and the paint marks on the exterior where the outside toilet was located.

Unless there was an event going on in Ickham I didn't get to mix with the local children, my playmates were uncles aunts and grandparents and one of my cousins, who lived with my paternal grandparents.

On occasions I would see new people, the telephone company needed to erect a new pole in our garden, I of course supervised its arrival at the tender age of five, they rewarded me when they left by giving me a chocolate banana for all my hard work!

When I proudly showed my mother, she explained through floods of laughter that it was a very over ripe and inedible banana, still to this day I keep my eyes open to catch them to exact revenge! It was only in recent times I worked out they would be about 115 years old now!

I met a local family who lived in Treasury view at an event at the village hall, they were about four years old to my tender six years. Just a few days later I would meet them again.

I was allowed to roam Hazelden woods at the rear of the house at will, as long as my mother knew where I was. I was free to mooch around playing games in my head and making dens etc.

One day I was going down towards Duckpitts farm along the old logging track in the wood, when I heard the sound of crying a hundred yards or so inside the wood in a particularly dense part. It was quite dark and quite foreboding as the sun couldn't break through the tree canopy. These days the wood has gone replaced by soft fruit orchards.

On getting nearer I discovered it was the two children I had met a few days earlier. They were lost and didn't know where they were. I took them home and after some milk and biscuits, mum walked them home.

We had a small car, an Austen Seven which was Dad's pride and joy, I can still remember the plate now ALY123! It replaced an older model which its demise I witnessed as I describe further on. We used to go to the garage along Wingham road known as 'The Casino Garage'.

Dad was born at Grove and moved to Bramling aged one day old, he used to tell stories of the events and dances that were held in the dance hall behind the garage during his teenage years.

The forecourt had two petrol pumps and a strange pump with a knob that you could twist to obtain the correct ratio of two stroke oil. There was another hand-held pump with a handle grip where you could ask for 'two shots' It was called Redex. It was a type of oil and bright pink in colour.

I had no idea what it was for then but more recently, I discovered was a type of oil to make the cylinder head and piston rings work more efficiently.

Where you paid for your petrol was in the corner of a large room with many windows all around the outside. This was the dance hall which according to Dad, had seen its fair share of riotous behaviour over the years.

There was a part time café in the corner where you could get a cup of tea and a bottle of pop! In the centre was the shiniest thing I had ever seen. It was an American juke box, full of the latest records. It seemed massive to a youngster; it was bright red in colour with mainly chromium facings which was polished as if it had just arrived from faraway places.

You could see the records standing vertically on a circular track with an index and corresponding number ready for the button to be pressed.

Every now and again Dad would stop for a tea and someone would put a penny in and music would blare across the forecourt and beyond.

Dad would always say it wasn't like it used to be, the dances in his day were live bands playing the music of the 30s/40s through to the mid 1950s.

The jukebox loaded up of the latest rock and roll records was a step too far for him to bear! It was here that the young Fred Bennett returned from his service in the Royal Air Force and that very same night, attended a dance there and met a young Gladys Garrett! The rest of course is history.

When I started my apprenticeship there many years later the jukebox had been relegated to the rear of the building under a blanket. One day it disappeared and I never found out where it went to!

Parents can be quite cruel without realising it, even if it's for the best intentions. One Sunday morning in the spring, mum put a joint in the oven and we went out for a ride in the car.

We passed daffodils and snowdrops on the verges and eventually we stopped at a field where there were some new born lambs. Some were only a few hours old, they were playing in the sun and having a grand old time! We then went home and lunch was finished off ready to serve.

I casually asked what we were having and was proudly told 'we have roast lamb this week'! I didn't eat lamb again until my mid 20s!

One Sunday morning I suppose Dad was instructed to take me out so mum could prepare lunch in peace. We drove to Ickham in the car and collected my grandad. We then drove to one of the farms locally and collected Dad's old car. We towed grandad steering the old car noisily back to Bramling very slowly.

Dad had owned this car for some time but it was always breaking down and costing quite a bit of money, so its time was up! We turned up the lane next to the Volunteer pub, now of course named the Haywain!

After about half a mile there was (and still is) a chalk pit on the right-hand side. In those days the chalk pit was only separated from the road by a small strip of grass about twelve inches across and then a sheer drop.

We stopped adjacent to the edge and I was instructed to remain in the car. The two grownups undid the rope and with much sweating and heaving, pushed the old car over the edge into the pit. I was allowed to inspect the result. The car was upside down in the bushes below.

A few years later, when I was allowed out on my bicycle on my own, I often rode down past the chalk pit and looked at the car, disappearing out of site in the rapidly growing bushes and trees.

Now there is a raised verge, a barbed wire fence and those small bushes and trees have grown into large structures towering way above the road. No sign of the rusting hulk below! It also occurred to me that Grandad didn't pass his driving test until I was a teenager! Oops!

One Sunday morning Dad said that we were going to look at a hole. Nothing exciting about a hole I thought and very disinterested, we walked across the road the through the farm out to the fields.

I would say at this point to set the scene that Bramling is a hamlet set in a small geographical feature known as a re-entrant. The soil is clay based but covering a chalk bedrock.

The hole in question was a Dene hole, its origins and use go back centuries but they are not very common. In Kent it seems that they have a shaft dug down several metres, leading to an underground cave complex.

The assumption was that they were built as a type of cold storage in pre–Anglo Saxon times. The one in question, became visible when the clay covering the entrance collapsed, following a period of prolonged rain revealing the caves underneath.

The locals took a ladder and all the grownups took it in turns to go down and inspect the hole. As a six-year-old, I was not allowed to go inside only look from the top, which I thought was completely unfair.

After various archaeologists and specialists looked at it, it was covered over and the field was re planted and I suspect that it has been forgotten about and never revisited. I could probably find it now but I wouldn't put money on it!

Holidays to the Bennett family in my early years was a once-a-year event. We used to visit my maternal grandfather's sister, Aunt Gladys at the pub she and her husband ran in the small village of Market Deeping in Lincolnshire.

This visit incorporated a visit to her father, Charles. Charles had lived in Folkestone all his life until his house was destroyed in 1940 by a German cross channel shell. He went to live near his daughter near the pub which he really enjoyed. Fred had lived next door to a pub in Folkestone!

The journey to Market Deeping took all day, motorways were non-existent then, with A and B roads being the only routes. The Dartford crossing hadn't been built so it was a trip into the east end of London and on to the A10, one of the major roads back then.

Tea break was always at the old airfield at North Weald where Dad was based after his basic training in the RAF. This was always a trip down memory lane for Dad, both parents served in the RAF during the war and held fond memories for their time in uniform.

Our lunch stop was always in the same place on these journeys, there was an RAF base at Bassingbourn. In the Second World war it was a US air force base that had B17 heavy bombers stationed there.

The site was downsized after the war when the Americans left and the road was reinstated. There was a parking area opposite the hangers where we would stop and eat our sandwiches whilst watching aircraft movement.

I was excited to see the first GR1 Harriers there and the sight of aeroplanes taking off vertically a hundred yards away was a sight to behold. We often brought great grandad back to Kent with us at the end of the holiday, to see his son and the rest of the family.

I remember this very well as the journey took what seemed to me a lifetime, great grandad wanted to stop at every pub all the way back to Kent!

Unbeknown to my parents, my uncle Dennis thought I needed a dog as company as there were no children around the hamlet for me to play with. I am not sure how he came to this conclusion as he lived in Thornton Heath near Croydon, and rarely came home.

So, on Christmas eve in 1962 he arrived home clutching his case, armfuls of presents and a puppy who refused to walk!

The journey from Croydon encompassed three train journeys and a number 13 bus from Canterbury! Laddie the Highland collie had arrived.

The snow started around Christmas eve that year and went on to March 1963, a snow blanket covered the UK and it kept coming together with extreme cold and biting winds.

Laddie and I played in the garden in the snow he was able to pull my little sledge along with ease and we had quite a bit of fun.

The winter of 1962/1963 was one of the coldest on record, our house was heated by one coal fire in the lounge, and the bedrooms were so cold that icicles hung down from the inside of the window frames, the outside toilet was a challenge as it was quite a few steps away from the back door.

I remember looking up and either seeing a crystal-clear sky, bluer that I have ever seen but so cold it froze my gloves, or the sky so dark and snowing, that twelve inches would fall consistently within a few minutes.

Of course, at the tender age of five the reality of this passed me by, Dad had to do deliveries to outlying areas where people were running out of supplies. He would often not get home until after midnight completely exhausted but be gone again before I had my breakfast.

He strapped the sledge to the roof and drove the van as far as he could and then walked for miles dragging the sledge piled high with boxes of groceries.

Eventually the delivery lorries couldn't get to the shop and the siege mentality experienced just a few years earlier, set in and everyone accepted they were in for the long haul with the weather.

I do remember that I didn't see a car on the road outside for days and this was the main road to Sandwich. It seemed so quiet and tranquil, a memory I hold vividly to this day.

This sense of tranquillity I was reminded of when serving in the forests of West Germany in the 1980s. I would stand and look out from the edge of the wood line, looking across the valley whilst the snow drifted down when the Cold War still threatened, and be reminded of those childhood days.

The total peace and quiet was itself extremely loud, the only noise audible were your own heartbeats. I often try and work out why I seemed to be at home during my early childhood, but I believe that I was always ill with various strains of viruses.

I looked at my mum's diaries some twenty years ago and was shocked at how ill I was. I had a weak chest when I was small, having asthma, this weakened my lungs so I had pneumonia several times (I am still susceptible to this even now), whooping cough, mumps, measles, German measles, chicken pox, influenza and various illnesses that didn't seem to have a name.

These would come and go and my body didn't build up immunity until I was ten or eleven, so these illnesses would have returned over and over again.

We worked out I missed over half of my primary education through illness. I still struggle with basic grammar, capital letters and correct punctuation to this day. Thank goodness for Microsoft Word spell checker!

It's strange how much certain memories remain with you throughout life. One day before we moved to Ickham, Dad came indoors and said 'don't move' there is a pheasant in the garden. I was intrigued with the prospect of a pheasant in the garden, whatever a pheasant was!

Dad fetched his single barrel shotgun from the cupboard and proceeded to stalk the pheasant that was happily wandering around the lawn, Mum and I watched from indoors and there was a huge bang and the pheasant took off vertically and disappeared over the trees complaining loudly.

Mum looked down at me and said in a very resigned tone 'he is useless with a gun' and went back to the kitchen.

A very despondent grocer came back into the house lamenting that he was such a good shot in the RAF, so why could he not hit a bird. Only years later it occurred to me that this was going to be supper and missing it meant we had to have omelettes again.

I remember we had about a dozen hens just inside the orchard at the top of the rear steps to the house. They were brown farmyard hens which produced eggs for all the extended family around us.

I used to help feed them but one of them always pecked the back of my ankle and chased me around the run, I do suspect we eventually had that one for lunch one Sunday!

In recent years we have owned hens and realised just how funny they can be including the gentle pecks you sometimes get. I get why it hurt the skin of a five-year-old, they can be a bit feisty when food is around!

There were a few cherry and apple orchards locally where the wives would earn money in the autumn. I remember the ladders used in the cherry orchards quite vividly. They had a wide span at the base but one third up they narrowed in a gentle curve until reduced their width by two thirds. They were only about twelve inches wide at the very top.

Colonel Friend at Duckpitts farm had one of these orchards almost opposite his house and mum, as I mentioned earlier was his housekeeper, picked cherries in the afternoons.

As a small boy of I guess, five, I joined the other children and played in the orchards on the random straw bales scattered around the area. I didn't realise these were for the modesty of the workers if 'they needed to go' during the day.

I remember being collected from the orchard by my grandmother one afternoon as mum had disappeared. It transpired she had fallen off the top of a ladder and broken her arm. I was totally oblivious of all of this fuss. No ambulances back then, she suffered the indignity of going to the hospital for attention sitting on the back of a trailer towed by an old tractor!

In the summer of 1964, we prepared to move to Fern cottage which had become vacant next to the shop. This was handy for Dad and work and set the scene for when my parents took the business on just a few years later.

I used to play with a boy opposite whose family worked for Edward Kerr on the farm in Bramling. The youngest boy, Keith was quite a few years older than me but he seemed fine.

One particular day he came around and suggested we play up in the orchard. As we were packing up getting ready to move, mum was pleased to have me out of her hair for a while and readily agreed.

A game of cowboys and Indians was set and after a while we went further up the orchard and played in the sheep pen. Part of the game was me being tied to a sheep wattle, playing the part of a captured cowboy.

This seemed fine until Keith said he need to go but would be back in a few minutes. He went home and just before he went out of the gate mum spotted the top of his head going by the window.

After a while I didn't appear so she came looking for me and was horrified that I had been tied firmly to the wattle around the neck, wrists and ankles. By this time the baler twine had cut in and left marks around my neck which were visible for weeks.

Mum took me across the road and left me with my grandparents while she went and 'had a little chat' with Keith's mum. Needless to say, I didn't see him again!

Ickham church from the South East

Chapter two. The move to Ickham village

When we moved to Fern Cottage both my parents then worked for the Coombs brothers, Dad having worked there since the early 1940s. They took over the business in 1971 when the Coombs brothers retired.

You could buy anything in the shop and if they didn't have the item, they would go out of their way to get anything you wanted the following day, and deliver it to your house at no extra charge.

The shop sold copious quantities of paraffin which people used for heating in it some outlying areas, this was also for lighting as well high-pressure Tilley lamps, and storm lanterns were still quite prolific in the early 1960s.

Back in 1964 the village was very much a rural farming community, nothing much had changed in the area since the early part of the twentieth century. The now open fields of crops ranging from wheat, barley and potatoes were the stock crop in our area.

It seems hard to imagine even so soon as the end of the First World War, the fields all around the area would just be hop gardens.

Just in the parish of Ickham there was fourteen Oast houses whose sole purpose was to dry and process hops for the brewing industry which even locally, could take more hops than the area could supply.

The Presland's who lived at Ickham hall, and the Hayward's from one of the local farms took their children to the same school I attended in Ash, so I hitched a ride with them until I went to Sturry Secondary school.

The house in Ickham was much larger and had a bathroom and two toilets, this was to a seven-year-old complete state of the art. There was a coke burning boiler in the kitchen to heat the hot water, but to my recollection the only time it was lit it filled the house with black smoke and left soot residue on all exposed surfaces and fabric!

The house was full of rubbish and old newspapers when we moved in, I was allocated a bedroom and when I opened the cupboard door it contained a pith helmet. This would have belonged to the previous occupant Mr Sidders, a former officer in the Buffs who spent quite a bit of time in Mesopotamia and India back in the day.

The only heating was a very efficient coal fire in the living room. Just outside the back door was a large shed type building where the coal was kept. The hot water was via an electrically heated tank in the airing cupboard, but only at weekends!

One thing that struck me was how light and airy the village was, having lived in Bramling where the house was very dark all the time. There were mature trees to one side whilst the house nestled in a hollow with a steep bank to the rear.

In Ickham the sky seemed so big, on a clear day after bedtime I would sit at my bedroom window, looking over the fields towards the west at the rear of the house, marvelling how the sky would change colour from blue to shades of red, likened to the glowing embers of a dying fire.

The glow would light up the back wall on my bedroom, bathing the room in a warm and comforting glow. This would diminish and finally vanish until darkness fell and the stars would appear.

There were no double-glazing windows back then, they were traditional sash windows in need of some TLC. In the summer I used to have my bedroom window open at the bottom and as my bed was directly underneath, could hear clearly the noises of the cars going from Littlebourne to Wingham in the distance.

The rumbling of motorcycle engines and lorries would be a steady drone. No high-pitched engine noise of the Japanese two stoke engines woke the night air. It would be another ten years before these machines would start to depose the traditional British four stroke machines, that had dominated for three generations.

These days aircraft noise above is the norm, with the sky full of aircraft moving in all directions as high at forty thousand feet day and night. Passenger aircraft during the day and freight traffic at night.

In the early 1960s the majority of aeroplane movement was still traditional propeller driven aircraft. I used to lie in bed and listen to the cargo planes probably from Southend Airport, a major freight hub then, flying to Le Touquet in France with the nightly shuttle of goods and exports.

The aircraft would just become audible and I would listen to them becoming louder and more of a resonance from the multiple engines. They would go overhead at around fifteen thousand feet with their strobe lights flashing.

The aircraft noise would diminish slowly, just before it vanished completely, you could just hear the slowing of the engines as it started its descent into Le Touquet.

Moments later you would repeat the process with another coming into hearing range. This would go on until daybreak. Interestingly, you never seemed to have more than one aircraft in the sky at any time, life in the sky seemed to mirror life in our idyllic rural community.

The garden extended back to the field belonging to the Church Commissioners, which was about a hundred yards to the back hedge. The garden in Bramling, was tiny and dark completely unsuitable for vegetable production, so Dad set about growing copious amounts of vegetables and soft fruit in this vast open space.

Given the hours he worked I am amazed he found the time to do the garden to such a high standard.

We had many birds in our garden, from the ubiquitous house sparrows which dust bathed in the area behind the lawn, to a pheasant which roosted in the large apple tree at the end of the garden.

We shared the gardens with the Coombs brothers with no dividing line so the view was extremely open plan, with low bushes, tidy beds and mature apple trees.

Our hen house came with us from Bramling but was never again used to house chickens. It eventually became an object of play and as I became older, I used to sit on the roof surveying the fields over the top of the hedge.

My love of all thing's nature was developed at this point I think, I used to count the nests in the hedges and list the species of birds. One year we had three linnet nests producing eleven fledglings.

There were house martins under the gutters just above my bedroom window producing a constant chatter and hubbub.

Blue, Great and Long tailed tits nested all around the sheds and buildings around the back of the shop next door, and the obligatory blackbird perched precariously in a nest on the rafters of the oil store, year after year.

We had grey squirrels in the garden during the late summer, feasting on the cobnuts which were prolific in the Coomb's side of the garden. Frank Coombs was always in the garden, shooing them away as he used to sell the nuts in the shop and they were eating his profit!

There always seemed to be more traffic on the road than there was in Bramling, being a farm community there was a constant stream of farmers land rovers, tractors and farm implements, going noisily past the house during the hours of daylight apart from Sundays.

Car ownership was still not the norm in the village, you could look down the street on a Sunday and there would be few parked cars. Most of the customers to the shops, pub and undertakers, either walked or cycled from around the area.

The biggest source of employment in the area was farming. The majority of the labour force lived in the tied cottages linked to the various farms, Hood's in New Place, Wyant's up school lane, Mayes at Treasury Farm, Hayward's at Ickham court,

Twyman's fruit farm and Montgomery's adjacent to the church in Wickhambreaux, Kelsey's, in Grove road, Burt's in Stodmarsh and Kerr's in Bramling etc.

At harvest and planting time you would hear in the early morning before the mist had lifted, the sounds of the tractors and trailers moving the groups of workers to and from the fields, crisscrossing the village to get to the days toil.

The gentle chatter of the workers could just be heard above the rhythmic engine note as they passed by. Regardless of the weather, they would be in the fields all day, carrying their drinks and lunch with them.

The mill in Wickhambreaux stopped milling flour during my memory, but the building and outbuildings were used by many small businesses, Sid Walters and his son's ran a manufacturing business making over the years rubber pouches, angle poise lamps, camping showers and curling tongs amongst other items over the years.

This eventually closed and an art school among other businesses took over the sheds.

The forge in Ickham was always busy doing agricultural repairs and frequent horse shoe replacements, although the horses were only owned as recreational animals in my early years.

In years gone by, the majority of horses would have been working animals where the importance of keeping their shoes in good condition, was an intrinsically essential part of the local farming businesses.

The Duke William back in the early 1960s through to the late 1970s, was the centre of the community in the evenings with the public bar serving the local workers, Fremlins mild and bitter in copious amounts after a hard day's harvest.

In the separate saloon bar, the tenant farmers and their wives would enjoy a quiet drink with the local professionals, listening to their raucous and high-spirited neighbours.

The door to the saloon bar had a small area where residents would pop in for crisps and take away jugs of beer. This little area was the only place an unaccompanied child could enter on an errand from a tired parent, for non-alcoholic goods.

In my memory, I recall the brewers dray being horse drawn, and the workers clad in leather overalls heaving barrels of beer into the beer hatch with ease followed by a pint of their finest, before moving on to the next pub.

This scene I imagined going on all day with tired draymen staggering home to their wives, worn out from the heavy lifting and intoxicated by all the beer!

The Rose Inn in Wickhambreaux mirrored this. Jock and Mary Wilson had a separate saloon bar, a billiards room and a small meeting room at the rear of the property. The workers from Montgomery's and

Twyman's used to frequent the public bar, whilst the local professionals would sit in the small saloon bar.

A real sense of community existed in those days; the village halls always had events and activities, the fetes and flower show on the village greens were always well supported and the churches well attended.

Tucked away towards gutter street was another pub the Hooden Horse, this was quite small but hosted probably the most exciting event in the farming calendar. I have already mentioned the amount of hop gardens there used to be around the parishes, at the end of the hop picking the medieval tradition of Hop Hoodening, was performed outside on village greens and local pubs in villages across East Kent.

This was no different in Wickhambreaux, the road outside the pub was closed and Morris dancers would perform with a wooden horse's head on a pole, was paraded and cheered on by the local residents.

When I was about fourteen, I was allowed to go and watch this event, it was usually on a Saturday evening so no time restraints for school. The pub was very strict with the licencing laws, so all the children gathered in a back room whilst the adults partied in the two small bars, spilling out into the road until closing time.

On a more unsavoury note, all the properties in the village had a cesspool, it wasn't until about 1970 did mains drainage appear through the village, but a bit more on that in a moment. The cesspools were emptied by the local council.

A burgundy-coloured lorry would be around the villages driven by the same guy who had worked for the council for years!

He would connect up and switch on the pumps and sit in his cab eating his sandwiches and read the paper. I can't remember him using gloves and his overalls had a hue about them. I used to visualise him living by himself and pitied his near neighbours!

One year we had a big summer storm and unbeknown to anyone, there was a deep underground water course running underneath the village.

Suddenly all the cesspits were empty, the storm had caused a flood underground and washed away the bottoms of the cesspits.

In days gone by these were wells used for drinking water. Most of them had a brick wall lining and were thirty feet deep or there abouts at the top end of the village, and half that down by Rectory cottages.

Clearly the underground stream had been the water supply for the village until piped mains water arrived in the early twentieth century.

We had been in plan for mains drainage for years, but recent events jumped us up the queue due to the contamination risk. The teams closed the village in stages, with huge mechanical diggers digging down in readiness to lay the pipes.

Along the pipe route the underground stream was exposed. When it was exposed the sound of running water was amazing, twenty feet down you could see clear water and fine gravel, sometimes you could see a channel with an air gap above clearly a long-standing stream.

The task took longer and experts had to make sure the new pipes didn't block the course of the existing underground river course. Eventually all the houses were connected up and the red tanker was never seen in the village operationally again.

The driver did call into the shop daily to pick up supplies, I remember mum going around afterwards spraying air freshener like a demented maniac!

The cesspools were sealed over and in recent years after the arrival of water meters, some residents used their old wells for watering their gardens. I would like to think they didn't know the story of the underground stream under their garden, and the flood which caused havoc!

The supermarket was unheard of until the late 1980s so the villages supported several small independent shops. In Wickhambreaux, the Llewellyn family had a general stores and post office opposite the mill, an antique shop opposite the Rose owned by an emotionally troubled Mrs Pestel.

When I was a late teenager Mrs Pestel took her own life by gassing herself in her old grey minivan in Trenley Park wood!

There was a bakery run by Mr Giles with its tea rooms attached which supported four villages and the rural area out to Preston and Westmarsh, with fresh bread daily.

A sweet shop and an electrical contractor, Mr Rye who occupied properties and a yard in gutter street (when it had a convex surface and the water ran down the centre of the road into the dyke at the bottom of the List).

Back then the security for the electrical yard was a piece of rope strung across two small posts! Even a dachshund could jump in at the centre, such was the lack of bandits around at that time.

The cottage next to the village school was converted into a tea room and became very successful attracting coaches from all around the area in the summer months.

Derek (Del) and Peggy Bower ran the business successfully for many years. Peggy was related to the Morelli family of ice cream fame in Broadstairs.

I remember there was a builder, Len Masters who managed to make a living without going out of the village. Len had a wooden leg but no one was brave enough to ask how he lost the original one!

In Ickham the village stores were owned by the Coombs family, they delivered groceries as far as Patrixbourne, Bekesbourne, Westmarsh and Grove.

You could buy wellies and plimsoles together with hand weighed loose flour, dried fruits and all you could possibly want. Even gentleman's relish was stocked for the more discerning clients.

There was an agricultural merchant opposite the church which eventually downsized and became a small sweet shop. My first flying saucers and liquorice was purchased there with my pocket money!

There was a sweet shop at the bottom of the village but this closed before we moved to Ickham. An undertaker Albert White, was in between Treasury farm and Carpenters lodge working most days in the week.

Albert together with Bob Curling who lived in Wingham, hand made the coffins so there was always activity going on in there.

The sounds of sawing and planing was emanating from the double doors at the front of the building when you cycled by. Bob was a skilled carpenter and when they weren't making coffins, Bob would produce some large handmade dressers and furniture for the local residents at a fraction of the cost of the specialist shops in Canterbury.

Many years later when I was doing my apprenticeship at the Casino garage on the Wingham road, the garage owner came rushing into the workshop and asked me to drop everything and go and front lift Albert White's estate car as a matter of urgency.

I arrived a few moments later to find the engine had blown up. On inspection there was a loaded coffin in the back! I lifted the car and took it complete with undertaker to Wingham church where due diligence was done. I then towed the car back to the garage!

Such are the memories that stick with you for ever. I can still remember who was in the coffin but that information I will keep to myself!

There were some eccentric characters around the village, one of these was the butler working at Escomb, the big house opposite the pond. His name escapes me but he was clearly an ex-sergeant major who walked upright, and carried his umbrella as if it was the ubiquitous pace stick, harping back to his military career.

One year the general election canvassing was in full flow, the local conservative MP was Sir David Crouch who was popular and a successful local MP. Needless to say, the shop delivered his groceries and he ran an 'account'

There were blue posters in people's gardens and in windows. Mr Coombs had a huge poster which spanned both our front gardens. The butler marched down to the shop for his daily paper and supplies when he suddenly bent over and walked past our house crouching down.

This happened for a couple of days when it became apparent the butler was obeying instructions. The sign said CROUCH so he did!

I spent a great deal of time with my great aunt Phoebe, she, to a small child seemed very old, she was one of fifteen children, she was born in 1900, and looked ancient. Phoebe lived in Cherville cottages overlooking Ickham, a short walk on the way to Bramling.

She had worked in service as a youngster and then on the farms until she retired. She was a slight built lady but strong as an ox and fit as a fiddle with a broad Kentish accent, a cross between Devon and Suffolk with a mixture of Sussex!

One day she arranged with my mum to go and see her sister-in-law, aunt Daisy in the village of Elham. On the face of it this seemed fine but the reality was a cross country bike ride, Bramling, Barham and beyond.

Pheobe's bike was as old as she was, but it went like the wind and I struggled to keep up with my small bike with no gears. After some lunch it was time to ride home and by now it was raining! I would have not undertaken that journey in my 20s. let alone at nine years old. Every muscle ached for days.

A few days later we did another trip this time to Goodnestone to see another sister-in-law, great aunt Dolly. This was considerably nearer but I had barely recovered the use of my legs and this was also tortuous. After this when a visit was on the cards, I would not feel very well and she had to go on her own.

When she became a bit frail, she moved into Forge House and my mum and brother Dennis, kept an eye on her for many years. Phoebe lived until grand old age of 93, passing away in the nursing home in Wickhambreaux.

Laddie the Collie

Chapter three. Adventures

Childhood was fun in the villages once I got to know everyone, we would all congregate on the village green in Wickhambreaux playing games on the green, and exploring the abandoned chicken farm where the community field now stands.

Trips to Deadmill bridge down the river and playing around the pill boxes became the norm. Cricket and ball games on the green at Ickham in the summer, attracted the local children aged from barely able to walk to mid teenagers, we all got on together and looked out for each other.

The old river course remained dry and one day I decided to walk it from Seaton back towards Littlebourne. This was quite a feat for a ten-year-old as the cows to me then looked enormous, but I always checked for the bull first!

Just before I reached Wickham lane, I noticed a few fossils set into flint nearby. When I stopped to collect them, I saw a stone age flint axe and a small sharp tool inches, from where I was kneeling. The axe was about eight inches long and it still resides in my loft now.

I consider that I am the caretaker of it and given its age, it probably should be in a museum. This incident inspired my love of history, I visualised the inhabitants of the area during the stone age using the old river as a source of water, while they passed through as seasonal hunter gatherers, stopping to rest preparing their food and settling down for the night.

It was not until I was well into my teens, did I realise that the area between the villages was part of the estuary of the Wantsum Channel, which separated East Kent from the Isle of Thanet.

The place where I found the stone axe would have been part of a tidal area, with the inhabitants foraging and catching fish and small mammals along the shoreline. There was even water of some depth up to Seaton mill in the Middle Ages, as it's recorded that Seaton was the port for Ickham.

As you go along the river towards Littlebourne, the river crosses the road near Riverside cottages, and there is a small field on the north side of the river. Harry Twyman used to keep his pigs in the field there. As youngsters we used to go and sit on the safety rail and watch them for hours.

One of my friends said he was a 'pig expert' and could make the pigs go to sleep. We were fascinated with this and asked him to explain. He picked up a stick and leaned into where the pigs were standing in the shade.

He proceeded to rub the stick on the base of each animal's tail. After a few moments the pig laid down and went fast asleep. More animals were rubbed and one by one they fell asleep!

This was seriously good fun and every time we went down that way, and the pigs were near the road, we put them to sleep. One time we were leaning into the field, one of the farm hands came along and started to shout at us.

He thought we were hitting the pigs with a stick and quite rightly became upset. We tried to explain ourselves and he wouldn't listen to our reasoning.

Some hours later I had to explain to my dad and eventually I took him down there to show him what we were doing. We didn't do it again because of the angst it caused!

There never seemed to be a time constraint on what we did, we would randomly lay on a grass bank and stare up at the clouds forming, making shapes in your heads of random animals, this would lose an hour without really trying.

We would catch sticklebacks from the stream behind the school, putting them in jam jars and take them proudly home to our parents. The river had been diverted a few hundred years ago, to make it more convenient for the new mills built locally to process the grain. They needed to be near the road to take the grain to be milled and the flour away to the merchants across the county.

We found an old tyre in the river by Wickhambreaux mill, on closer inspection it contained several eels. This gave us an idea, after doing some research it was clear that some people actually do eat eels.

The Rose inn was prepared to pay a good price for a good-sized eel, so we acquired a few tyres from the local farms and proceeded to put them in the river at strategically placed spots, so we could recover them without getting too wet.

The following day we checked our traps and was thoroughly disappointed when they were found to be empty! We gave up on the idea, but about a week later someone suggested we go and check the traps.

We couldn't believe our luck, fifteen good sized eels equalled pocket money made for the weekly trip to the Saturday morning pictures at the ABC cinema in Canterbury, which this week, would include a bag of chips!

I remember hanging upside down on the bar on the entrance by the green, I wondered how many children have done this since, as the same bar is still there after all these years!

We used to make rafts and float down the river from the mill, tickling trout and throw bread into the river for the mallards which used to congregate in the millpond.

What struck me recently was the lack of damage, vandalism and noisy behaviour we exhibited. I think the worse thing I did was to let off a stink bomb in the toilets of the Rose, when they were located on the outside of the building!

I think we were lucky have been children during the 60s and the 70s, life was so much easier and simplistic for youngsters then, no social media, mobile phones or influencing television.

We did our own thing, amused ourselves whilst our parents were working. School holidays were a dream, you went out early in the morning with an apple and a sandwich, returning tea time, starving hungry, filthy and tired.

Small groups of children used to congregate either around the village greens in Ickham or Wickhambreaux, where we used to chat play ball games, and generally amuse ourselves.

Something you just don't see today is a group of children sitting on a gate doing nothing. We used to sit on top of the five-bar gate at Seaton, chatting and absorbing the nature around us.

The sky would be blue with fluffy clouds and the gentle hum of bees and flying insects permeating the air. Sparrows in profusion, would be bickering and jumping around in the hedge, and the distant sound of rooks cawing in the wood, a short walk away.

The smells on the breeze would awake the senses, the smell of grass being mown drifting in the air, the smell of the shiny brown cows just in front of us, to the occasional scent of fat hen would all add to the conversation.

I think children of my era were more aware of the country and tuned into nature than they are today, the open spaces seemed to go on for ever.

We used to look around the local churches and try and link names on the gravestones to family names in the village. We were always amazed at the ceiling in Wickhambreaux church, the gold stars painted onto the blue background was incredible for a village church.

We were in awe finding the grave of one of the WW2 flying heroes, David Maltby, one of the Dambusters of 617 squadron, who's relatives lived in the village during those troubled times.

Buried in Ickham churchyard was a gentleman who had fought at the Battle of Waterloo, his family had lived at Lee Priory during the Peninsular war. As children we would research these individuals at the Beaney library after our weekly trip to the ABC cinema on Saturday mornings.

One week we had excitement in the villages, the word was out that there was to be a recording for the local ITV magazine television program 'Scene South East' down by the river in Wickhambreaux.

A reporter was going to do a piece on camera down by the mill and there would be a helicopter flying along the river. On the day of filming which coincided with the summer holidays, we wandered down to Wickhambreaux to see what was going on.

The plan was the helicopter would fly from Seaton to Littlebourne along the river at treetop level as the opening credits rolled. They wanted some local children to be cycling along the road by Spicers place whilst they filmed.

We duly signed up and cycled up and down for hour whilst the helicopter went back and forward. The reporter did her piece to camera, we were thanked and parted company.

Just after the teatime news that Friday, I watched the television with great interest. Sure enough, there was the helicopter, travelling along accompanied by the Beatles hit 'Here comes the sun' as the helicopter arrived to the school, the scene jumped forward to the mill and there for a millisecond was the top of my head! And then it faded to the reporter!

I just don't have much luck with television, I was interviewed at Dover Castle by the BBC news for the twentieth anniversary of the death of Diana, Princess of Wales (the former Colonel in Chief of my regiment).

I was interviewed all morning and finally when the broadcast was put out on national television, I had three seconds of fame, just slightly better than before!

I had some friends living in Treasury cottage, opposite the Old Rectory at the bottom of Ickham street and next door in the new houses, so we used to congregate on the grass strip under the enormous Cedar of Lebanon adjacent to the Rectory.

We had to be careful, the owner of the Rectory, Alf Leggatt MBE had a massive peacock Charlie, which roamed the large gardens at will.

This peacock roosted in the cedar tree and wasn't tied by daylight hours. The bird didn't really like children and would show its displeasure by depositing carefully aimed liquid droppings, from twenty feet up the tree! We always had to check the tree before stopping to chat and even then, it would fly into the upper branches from behind the wall!

Whilst we are on the subject of Alf Leggatt, I must recount a story which is legendary to a certain generation. Alf had a well-stocked golden carp pond in the grounds of his property.

When I say pond, it was bordering on a small lake. We used to go around there and watch the fish swimming about lazily in the sun. One day the fish were starting to vanish and eventually they all disappeared.

Alf was convinced there was a pike or similar sized predator living in the pond. How it got there was a mystery but he persevered and restocked. Over a couple of weeks, they all vanished again. I would point out that we were in the middle of summer with very long days and endless periods of sunshine, this will be a factor further on.

Alf was well connected, and one morning my friend Richard called in and asked me to come down the village and something quite exciting was happening.

We rushed down there and to our surprise the village was full of military vehicles. Alf knew the legendary explorer and adventurer, founder of 'Operation Raleigh' the now famous outward-bound experience for youngsters, Colonel John Blashford-Snell.

He had arrived complete with his troop of Royal Engineers divers and explosive experts! To see this amount of hardware on Alf's lawn was great fun for us teenagers.

Eventually the diver couldn't find any evidence of the pike or its ilk, they decided that an explosion would shock any predator into submission and that would sort out the problem. There was a huge bang you could hear in Littlebourne and a plume of water fifteen feet high.

That sorted the problem, copious amounts of tea and biscuits were consumed and the Army retired to its barracks at Maidstone, a useful training exercise completed and Alf, at vast taxpayers' expense, had his lake cleansed of golden carp eaters.

Alf restocked his pond at considerable expense and nothing more was thought of the previous month's upheaval.

About a week later the golden carp again were disappearing, so a furious Alf was at the point of getting 'Blashers' back with a bigger bang, when one of the family noticed the very fat heron sitting by the lake just after daybreak one morning! The lake was netted over and the fish problem was finally solved.

One school holiday, I remember a group of us walked down the fields behind Seaton, this was years before the gravel was dug out to form the lakes, to the weir in the river. We played there for hours paddling and generally having fun.

One side of the weir was very deep and we stayed clear of this, but the lower side rippled and eddied so we would try and make dams and race leaves or sticks, in the fast-running water.

Many children joined us ranging from teenagers to youngsters of eight or nine. We did this for several days during that holiday, and the word got around so ultimately there was probably fifteen of us there.

There was also a weir on the tributary that came from the spring beyond Wingham down on the marshes below Britton farm. This was quite a walk, but there were more sticklebacks that part of the river there, worth the walk so we used to catch them with jam jar traps.

Again, a large group of the local children congregated there, being very careful to keep away from the deep side of the weir. We were fearless around water, I didn't learn to swim until I was sixteen, but water held little fear for me, I suppose I hadn't been near enough to it to give me any concerns.

I remember my parents approaching me quite sternly and asked if I had been down the weir below Britton farm the previous day, a young lad who was with us had drowned in the deep side of the weir, unbeknown to us he had gone back down there after we had gone home.

Trevor Rye was his name and I felt really bad that this had happened, and I have remembered the incident quite often over the years. He was with us as we cycled home past where he lived at Britton farm cottages and he went indoors, we didn't contemplate he would actually go back on his own. Trevor was only eight years old.

I used to spend a great deal of time with Grandparents, my paternal grandparents used to travel down to Deal quite frequently. They used to rent a caravan there for a week's holiday and more often than not, I would go too.

It was usually in the summer holidays so Mum and Dad didn't have to worry about me when they were at work. Dad's disabled sister, Eileen, my cousin Diane, and the grandparents would load up the car and take the trip to Deal quite often.

Sometimes we go just for the day and visit the seafront, wander down the pier which always guaranteed an ice cream in a cone from the Deal Beach Parlour, which is still there and trading after all these years.

There was an amusements hall with slot machines and the penny slide machines, where we could win pennies when the slide pushed them across the tipping point, when you slid the coins down a slide at the appropriate moment.

The day was always finished with fish and chips from the 'chippie', along the front at Walmer before a journey home.

Occasionally we would spend a week at the caravan park, and it was great fun crossing the golf course to play down by the beach with Laddie the collie.

One year, there was to be a summer fete held on the marshes between Wickham lane and The Drill. There had not been one for some years and this particular year the two villages combined efforts and it was due to be amazing.

As youngsters we used to clip a piece of stiff cardboard to the rear frame of our bicycles with an old clothes peg. If you adjust it correctly so it flicked the spokes on the rear wheel, it sounded like a motor bike if you use your imagination to its full potential.

I never rode my bike slowly anywhere and one particular day I had been up to Cherville to see my auntie Pheobe and deliver some vegetables from the garden.

On the way back down the hill I was getting up some speed and the cardboard was doing its job, but as I reached the village hall, something went wrong with my 'motor bike' and the noise changed. I looked behind me and, in an instant, ploughed into the brick wall.

I woke up in hospital later that day with concussion but what galled me more was how my friends came in to see me the day after the fete, telling me just how good it had been.

Coconut shy, music and dancing and hot dogs! I was peeved to miss the big event of the year. I was discharged after four days and told to rest. More school missed!

As you go down the marshes toward Deadmill bridge there was a small wood. A group of us would go down there camping in the summer, I was probably about twelve years old, cooking on a gas cooker bacon and eggs, and learning how not to put too much water into instant mashed potato was about as exciting as it gets, for a youngster living in the country during that innocent time in the early 1970s.

The night noises in the wood were quite comforting, some of my friends camping with us weren't so sure.

Living in Bramling with the woods at the end of our garden, reminded me of those early days and the creaks and groans of the trees rubbing against each other in the gentle breeze, together with passing animal noises were very comforting.

In the morning we would leave our tents and wander the marshes, we used to walk down to Wenderton woods and search for fossils in the bank.

The west side of the woods was completely barren. There was nothing on the ground nor leaves in the trees. This was a long-time roost for millions of starlings, that would fly around at dusk looking like a solid moving mass before eventually roosting in the trees.

The noise they made was deafening, my dad said they had been doing that since he was a child in the 1930s. In the early 1970s they suddenly disappeared. Within a couple of years, the wood recovered and you would never know they had ever been there.

Camping in the little wood was such fun, life was innocent and there seemed to be no limits imposed upon us. We cooked up instant mashed potato, tinned stew and processed peas, always being careful not to add too much water. There was nothing worse than sloppy potato!

During one trip, my parents visited with laddie the collie. A rare day out for them, as they walked back across the field, laddie jumped across a small dip in the field but this turned out to be a weed covered four feet deep ditch.

Suddenly the black highland collie was now a green, smelly and sulking dog. Dad said it took three hours to get him clean and dry.

My parents had driven down to Seaton and parked near the gate. Mum couldn't drive then so she drew the short straw and had to walk laddie home across the fields. This was the last time they visited my camping trips.

Nowadays there would always be an adult within earshot ensuring the children were safe. I am unsure that there were no more 'odd' people around then than now, or was the media not as advanced or focussed as it is now?

I recall we went by bicycle and left them at the gate on Seaton road, two days later they would be where we had left them, no thought of them being moved or stolen.

During our childhood we were not worldly wise, why should we be? These days we would be described as 'yokels' I was given a fly-fishing rod by one of my distant relatives. It came complete with a reel and quite a long amount of the heavy line you need for the weight to throw the fly where the fish may be hiding.

As a youngster I took the instructions quite literally, you tie the fly to the end of the line. I found a couple of dead house flies and duly tied them to the end of the line! My parents laughed until they cried!

Now many years later, I am now very adept at fly fishing and kitted out correctly!

I did find it difficult going to a different primary school to most of my friends, plans would be set for the weekend to which I would be blind, but in the main, I fitted in with whatever had been planned for the weekend.

I often discussed this with my parents over the years and they felt at the time it would not be in my best interests to move me given my sickness record.

In the school holidays it never seemed to rain, but I guess it did just as much as it does today, the river was always full.

My friend David who lived next to Wickhambreaux school came up with a plan one day. His parents owned the tea rooms and he decided that when it next snowed, we would go to the downs at Stodmarsh and use one of his parent's aluminium tea tray as a toboggan.

We did not have long to wait, that year the weather was awful. We went to the Christmas eve church service in Ickham, it was bitterly cold when we came of the door the path down to the lynch gate was covered in about an inch of snow.

The wind had dropped and the heavy snow had eased up, large and small flakes were drifting down gently, illuminated by the light above the church door. a strange silence hung in the air, so still and quiet, a very odd sensation.

The adults muttered and complained, but the children were excited about the prospect of a white Christmas without any thought of family movements and relatives visiting from distances, that would have caused problems and disruption the following morning.

My Aunt and Uncle and cousin Alan were staying with us and as the other family members were local it didn't affect us very much. I had little sleep that night, I kept looking out of the window at the ever-deepening snow.

Christmas day was fun as usual but we were not allowed to go outside and play in it. Boxing day was another matter, we were dispatched early to play in the snow. We went down and collected David and his tea tray and went up to the downs.

We met a few other children on route and the group of us walked up to Stodmarsh. No one else had been there before us on that day, the snow was crisp and pure.

A quick walk to the bottom of the hill to find the best route to take presented a problem, the barbed wire fence had been renewed during the year and this gave us some concern. It was very low just touching the top of the snow in some places.

We concluded that if we rolled off the tray at the bottom of the hill the tray would jump up and stop short of the wire. This worked well until it was my cousins turn, he was last to go and had watched all of us roll off at the bottom.

He sat on the tray but and for some reason touched the snow with his foot half way down, the tray changed course over untouched snow. When the time came to roll off, he didn't move despite shouts of encouragement, he hit a bump with the tray.

My cousin was flying over the top of the barbed wire fence and disappearing into the wood. Silence, not a word. The snow had the effect of depressing noise and our shouts went unanswered.

We rushed down the hill and went into the wood. Alan was still sitting on the tray in six inches of water in the river Lampen looking stunned. We congratulated him on his skill at managing twenty-five feet freestyle but he wasn't too impressed.

The snow game was cut short for us and we walked home with him sobbing, freezing cold and soaking wet. I of course was grounded for well over a week, plus many other sanctions which was painful as I love snow, and still do.

Watching from the window didn't do my morale much good at all. I don't think my cousin visited us again for some months either!

We repeated the tea tray toboggan over a few years as it always seemed to always snow in the winter then. It was unusual for us not to be snowed in at least once every year, we used to look forward to taking bets to see if the school buses would get through, we decided thirty minutes late was the cut off time and then we all went home.

There was the Sturry bus which came through Trenley woods which went to Sturry school and the East Kent Road car service bus which took the children to the Grammar schools in Canterbury.

If one came and not the other, bets were won and lost! thirty minutes later we would all be back out on the village green minus our uniforms dressed for the weather building snowmen and having snowball fights.

The parents of today would have had to take time off work or make hasty arrangements with grandparents, we just carried on!

Snow in Ickham always seemed so deep. I have photographs showing Baye lane completely buried in snow whilst at the same time, the level of snow on the fields was over twelve inches deep.

The pill box behind the church used to completely disappear in a huge mound of snow. One would hope that it wasn't like that in the winter of 1940/1941 when the South London Fusiliers manned it via a trench network, leading back down to the village green.

I read somewhere about a scandal regarding 'phone tapping', apparently this was a big thing in the USA. I as a naïve twelve-year-old made the wrong assumption of this 'very bad practice'. The old red phone box just outside our house had one of the early telephones, it had a button 'A' and a button 'B'.

To make the phone work you would lift the receiver and place the money into a slot adjacent to button 'A'. You would then dial the number, when the other person answered, you would press button 'A' and you could speak. If they didn't answer you would press button 'B' and your money was returned.

I lifted the receiver and tapped. Nothing exciting about this I thought, but then it came to me. If you tapped the lever in a rhythmic fashion ie, tap seven times and the machine would think you are dialling seven, you could make a call, yes, a bit long winded but it worked!

On the next trip to the Saturday morning pictures I tried it before I came home. If you tapped ten times it would dial a '0', so I furiously tapped 7...2...1...2...3...7 and my dad answered. I said I was just about to catch the bus.

On arrival home I was questioned as to why I called, I never called. I explained, and again both parents laughed and suggested I read all about the US Watergate scandal, and the true meaning of tapping would be revealed.

As very early teenagers there was really nothing to do in the villages for entertainment other than by our own amusement. A couple of the parents identified this and started a youth club in Wickhambreaux village hall on a Thursday evening.

This was a game changer for us, there were three distinct groups of children, the ones just about to start secondary school, the group who had been at secondary for about a year and finally, the group about to leave school.

Pam and Roland Epps took the time and investment to get all the children engaged and focussed at that time. I think all that group would agree, we are all better individuals thanks to them.

The good work was done for many years when they handed it over to Tony Young and Danny Foster who did a sterling job for a few years until work commitments forced closure.

As our group of teenagers approached the important exam years at school, some new families moved into the villages from outside the area. This changed the dynamics of the friendships, causing some distress and upset.

Some of the new youngsters were a little challenging, appearing on what would be on today's behavioural/conditional spectrums.

Examples of random vandalism and thefts began to take place around the villages which caused everyone to be under suspicion.

One incident really upset the youth club group, a set of records owned by one of my good friends were stolen and found smashed to pieces on the green at Wickhambreaux, it was not a good time to be a teenager.

As we were thinking about careers those families moved away again and things returned to the way it used to be.

Wickhambreaux church from the South East

Chapter four. Distractions

I developed an interest in radio which has remained all my life during my early teen years, I was given a transistor radio with a cream-coloured earpiece by my uncle when I was ten, and that was the key to a new world.

I was there at the end of pirate radio era, listening to Radio Caroline and Radio London on medium wave long after I should have been asleep.

After the Marine Broadcasting Offences Act in 1967 took all the pirates off the airways, I discovered on the long wave, radio Luxembourg on 1440 meters.

I marvelled at the music coming from so far away, made more authentic by the way it used to fade in and out due to atmospheric conditions. Kid Jenson and the 'Emperor' Rosko were becoming household names but you had to belong to the 'club', the group of your peers with ear pieces, discussing the music played in the playground from the night before.

My interest in communication led me to go to college one evening a week to learn how to be a member of the Radio Society of Great Britain by studying and passing the radio amateurs exams. This was just after I attained the age of fourteen.

It wasn't until nearly forty years later I actually used my callsign in earnest, following a second career in the Army facilitating my penchant of radio communications.

One of the skills I learnt at college was to build a basic radio, another of the things I learnt was to build a simple device to absorb radio wave energy. It was known as a lossy toroid.

It was simply eighteen inches of copper wire wound around a carbon rod, taped up exposing the wire either end to add a connector. A few years later I made many of them, after perfecting them during a period of trial and error.

Near to the villages was the RAF radar station on the hill behind the village of Ash. Every time the radar dish turned a blip would appear on the television or a 'whoosh' noise on a radio. After a while you became used to it, but it was always there and extremely annoying.

Probably the worst effect was on the rudimentary hearing aids. If you used your hearing aid and stood in a certain place, the blip was excruciating in the ears!

If you connected the lossy toroid 'in line' on your TV aerial or radio aerial it blocked out the blip with no signal reduction. I made and sold hundreds of them and topped up my pocket money.

Being a country boy, I was always out and about on the local farms, Mike Mayes who worked Treasury farm suggested I should apply for a shotgun licence and help keep the flocks of pigeons at bay, in return he would provide as many cartridges as I could shoot.

These days there are few flocks of pigeons around but back in the early 1970s, they were prolific. Everywhere you looked in the sky there would be pigeons, in particular, during the winter months.

It seemed odd that grownups should advocate a fourteen-year-old to own and use a shotgun unattended but again it was a different era.

Down in the marshes behind Britton farm the river used to flow past the increasingly growing lakes, the gravel extraction there was in full flow in the 1970s, the gravel company built the concrete road down to the area to cope with the heavy lorry movement.

The wild mallards used to fly parallel to the river and on a full moon provided some interesting wildfowl shooting, it was easy to shoot them but more complex finding them when they fell to the ground. All this done before I reached the age of fifteen!

I used to spend quite a bit of time with Mike Mayes' son Patrick. He was given a Series 1 land rover with the top and framework removed to use around the farm, we would bomb about using this in the fields at Britton farm and down the marshes.

Patrick was rationed on petrol, a Series 1 only does about twenty miles to a gallon on the road, significantly less off road, so mowers and other petrol driven machinery were drained to satisfy this beast. Great fun had by all!

I could drive a tractor and reverse a loaded trailer at the age of fourteen, not on the roads of course! I used to help out at harvest time, loading bales onto the trailers ready for the farm labourers to take to the barns and stack the following day.

This skill came in handy some years later, when I took my HGV class one test with minimal training due to this skill learned at an early age!

I have always had a love of cricket since an early age which pleased my parents. They could go to work and I would be sitting in front of the television watching the BBC.

A test match lasted five days and I would be glued to the set throughout that period with parents knowing where I was. I began to play at school but with poor coordination didn't really do too well.

One day Peter Brownbridge, a university lecturer who eventually became the vicar of the parishes, approached me to play for the Ickham and Wickhambreaux cricket team.

I jumped at the chance, we played at the Christchurch University sports ground along Stodmarsh road. We quite frankly we not very good, our players were from all backgrounds and ages, some of the older players were quite clearly very good players back in their day, but...

I realised after a while that the aim of playing cricket was not the actual game but the event in the pub afterwards. A good excuse for the guys to have a bit of bonding time away from the wives and families!

I discovered shandy at the age of fourteen and have hated it ever since!

When I was fifteen, I was given an old scooter. It had all the side panels removed but it didn't start. It looked like a part started project that had been abandoned. I spent hours in the small garage adjacent to our house taking it apart and repairing or sourcing parts to exchange the broken components.

When the scooter was repaired, I used to push it across to the fields, with the farmers permission rode it around all the tracks in the fields.

All the local village shops began to close in the early 1970s leaving only my parents' shop. The Coombs brother's family had owned the village shop for over two hundred years, but both Len and Frank were approaching retirement.

They offered the shop on an indefinite lease to mum and Dad which gave them little option. It was a straight choice, take on the lease or be made redundant. This also meant that we would have to leave Fern cottage which was owned by the Coombs family, effectively a tied cottage.

The smaller of the shop signs on the outer wall. You could see this clearly as you drove down the village.

Chapter five. The village shop

Mum and Dad built up the business, identifying the changing world of retail and adding new lines and services as they worked. Dad was the front man and mum did the books and finances and the now dreaded VAT which when it came in during 1973.

Back then it was complex, time consuming and any mistakes were punished with exorbitant fines. The visit of the infamous VAT man was notified by letter, in the best quality vellum stationary and signed off with a personal flourish!

At 10am the bespectacled employee of the Crown would arrive in a smart pin striped suit and a bowler hat. He would carefully remove his paperwork from the leather briefcase he carried, and would be taken to the area where the telephone was kept and orders phoned through.

The telephone was unplugged for a couple of hours so as not to disturb this officious and downright scary man. Dad would do his best to work as normal but mum had to stand just behind the inspector, ready for his requests for this or that piece of paper.

The monthly accounts leger always seemed of interest but it only ever contained the dates and totals from the customers' order books so the monthly account was easy to compile.

After spending three hours looking grumpy, he would conclude the days business and both parents would wait eagerly to look at the expression on his face.

If he looked grumpier, he would have found an error and debriefed them at length whilst wagging his finger. If he broke into a smile, then all was well and he was offered coffee!

The visit of the VAT man went from annually to about every three years, thus reducing the already high stress levels of both parents. It was only after several years did, they realise that the VAT man caught the bus from Canterbury and following his days' work, would adjourn to the Duke William pub until the next bus to Canterbury arrived!

Christmas was always a busy time in the shop. If you went in there it was like an Aladdin's cave of really exotic goods, unusual fruit and vegetables, decorations and lights around the beams and walls giving a bright and airy environment to make customers feel completely at home. I suppose he was a trend setter in today's standards, we see the shops at Christmas equally decorated and brightly lit everywhere you go.

Back in the 1970s this was not the norm in the shops outside of the big cities, the country still was recovering from the austerity from the 1940s.

Extra staff were employed for 'pin money' on the run up to Christmas, for extra deliveries and to help restock the shelves. This was usually the Saturday girls or some of the ladies who drove the van.

Dad had a Ford escort van and for their personal use, a Ford Escort estate followed by a Ford Sierra estate. Both vehicles were used all day every day getting orders out to customers on the run up to Christmas.

I don't know how they achieved it but due to some shrewd ordering, they didn't seem to ever have a glut of stock when they closed on Christmas eve at 4pm!

This was the only day they didn't cash up, Dad used to take the shop and the post office takings over to the house and the shop books were not touched until late on Boxing Day. Those two days were their only real rest time all year! The customer base increased and people came from miles away to shop and stock up for Christmas.

Mum used to cook whole gammons on our cooker in the house which they used to sell by the slice, it tasted absolutely amazing and it wasn't until long after they retired, did I manage to get the secret from mum.

She used to soak the gammons in cold water for 24 hours to remove the salt, then cook the gammons in plastic bags. The only thing added was two glasses of Harveys Bristol cream sherry, her favourite tipple!

Every Saturday morning an elderly couple drove down from Orpington, to get a pound of ham. They did this for years which was a true testament to the quality of the product.

Dad was a true entrepreneur, he would take orders for 'under the counter' items, as a trained butcher he would get cuts of meat which were only available through a butcher's shop or bottles of alcohol and spirit for which he certainly didn't have a licence.

A trip to the wholesaler at 6am would produce a van full of goodies hastily unloaded before it became fully daylight and the village awoke to its daily routine.

Dad had an arrangement with Paul Newton who owned the newsagent in Littlebourne. He would take orders for the daily papers, except for Sunday when he considered that to be his true day off.

Paul would have the papers ready and Dad would sort them in order and deliver them on the way home so the 'Gentry' and professional people could read them over breakfast.

Pension day was Tuesday, all pension payments were available from then onwards. Most of the local residents of pension age, would arrive at the door in a steady stream from the post office opening time.

At nine o'clock they would queue patiently outside. Dad would always make sure one of the part time staff was always working in the shop on a Tuesday morning.

After he paid the pensions, the customers would walk around the corner and they could buy their weekly goods.

It was like a military operation, probably the busiest day of the week. By lunchtime, everything calmed down. It was a good way to keep in touch with the residents, and usually you could find out how the more elderly residents were, by listening to the gossip as they all queued awaiting their turn.

The shop closed at 5.30pm but that was not the end of the day, my parents used to have their main meal lunchtime, mum used to sneak away to prepare something ready for the one-hour break at 1pm.

After they had closed for the day, they had a sandwich and a catch up on the news. They then both used to go back to work. Mum used to cash up whilst Dad did the daily accounting for the Post Office, they then used to put away all the perishables, clean down all the surfaces, sweep and tidy up. They would collapse exhausted at about eight o'clock most nights.

Wednesday was a half day in the area. Most shops would close and the shopkeepers would have a well-earned rest. After lunch we would take a trip to Deal or Folkestone have a walk around the pier or harbour before coming home late afternoon.

By 6pm they were back in the shop doing the normal daily routine. This was an unbelievable work ethic which no one outside our family even had an inkling.

As an early teenager I didn't get the way life evolved with the shop. I suppose there was an element of jealousy, suddenly I was left with relatives for longer periods during the day which to a fourteen-year-old, this gave a sense of being contained. Probably a throwback to my early years when I was always off school with illness.

Initially there was just the two of them in the shop, with my cousin Diane working part time after she left school. Eventually they would employ Saturday girls, Sharon Adams, Lee Hughes, Rosemary Brownbridge and Diane Cleaver to name but a few.

As the business developed, they employed a full-time storeman, van drivers and sales assistants. Clearly, they were doing well and able to provide employment for quite a few local people.

Within a month of opening they were burgled, but although the perpetrators couldn't access the sales area and safe because of the huge security bolts, they did clear out the hardware and the contents of the delivery boxes for the next day. A tremendous mess was made and damage to doors and windows caused issues a for a few days.

Most of the perishable goods were found in the hedge up school lane near the village hall. The burglar alarm was installed after this with a huge bell and blue flashing light on the outside wall in the street.

The storerooms of the shop where like a visit to a museum, above the sales area was a store room, which two hundred years earlier, had obviously been a bedroom with a small window overlooking the back gardens down the street. The glass was distorted and covered in years of dirt both inside and out.

The stairs to ascend were narrow and uneven, it was always difficult carrying up boxes and they general rule was to half empty the contents of a box downstairs, carry upstairs the remaining half, stack on the shelves and return for the remainder.

It had always been done this way and always would be! This was the dry goods store, shelves full of cereals, toilet rolls, spices, flour, 'ladies' products and a plethora of dry goods which wouldn't fit into the sales area.

Up until the early 1960s, most things came in bulk. Dried fruit would come in ten-pound bags, sugar in fifty-pound sacks, tea in the ubiquitous wooden chests etc. Dad used to say the Coombs brothers were so precise, he had to cut raisins in half to ensure they were the exact weight. 'It's the profit my lad, don't give it away!'

All of these loose goods would be carefully weighed out using aluminium scoops, worn away on the front edges from years of scooping (I guess we ate particles of aluminium but no health and safety back then!) The scoops and the weights from the scales are the few things I still have as a reminder of those times. The bags they used were blue paper, almost thin cardboard.

Above the lower stores was a double room full of hardware. All the wellies, plimsoles, electrical plugs, coat hooks, rope, chains, nails and screws were unearthed going back a very long time. Dozens of wicks and paraffin lamp lantern glasses, from a time before electricity was in the rural community.

An old-fashioned till was stored upstairs similar to the one used by the legendary grocer Arkwright in the popular TV program, 'Open all Hours'. It used to take your fingers off if you were not careful. I did use it several times before the electric one with accounting ability was installed.

In that store room everything had a layer of dust which seemed to have been there for ever. A place lost in time and space.

Every now and again someone would come in and ask if we had a certain 'widget' and after five minutes rummaging the 'widget' would be found and supplied with a smile!

In the first storeroom there was a bacon slicer, the fridges to store the bacon and cooked meat were behind it within easy reach. The slicing machine was a hand turned Berkel which was an amazing device. It was years old, painted bright red and had a blade as sharp as a razor.

Twice a year a man came to service and sharpen this beast! It had a dial on the side for controlling the thickness of the meat cut, 3 for ham and 5 or 6 for back bacon. Collar bacon was always cut on number 8!

As the world became more safety conscious, the rule makers decided that raw meat should not mix with cooked meat. This caused chaos, the old Berkel machine had been slicing bacon and ham in quick succession for years without anyone becoming ill. Now a new slicer and another fridge was needed!

Before health and safety came to Ickham the bacon joints were hung from the ceiling on traditional meat hooks, suspended from long redundant gas light pipes.

The temperature in that store never rose to more than 5^C even in the hottest summer, the winter was much colder. It is hard to imagine what the life was like in that part of the building when it was a house.

There was an old chimney breast in this store with what appeared to be a disused copper boiler set into the fireplace with enough air gap underneath to be able to light a fire.

I still to this day, have no idea what it was used for but during the heyday of the business, Dad used to keep whole stiltons in it as it was extremely cold on the run up to Christmas!

The availability of fresh vegetables was very seasonal, purchasing mushrooms at any other time than in autumn was unheard of. We would trudge the Adisham downs with baskets and a sharp knife collecting field mushrooms which would be sold the next day.

What the customers didn't know was when the mushrooms were picked, most had small worms which had burrowed up through the stem during growing. Dad used to lay them all out overnight upside down in the cool store area and in the morning would knock each one in turn on a box to shake out the worms which naturally burrowed upwards!

In the late 1970s a mushroom farm opened in the old farm estate in Littlebourne. There were a few old buildings shaped like the old war Nissan huts, probably left over from military occupation from the second world war.

You could buy closed cap, button and field mushrooms there in large punnets known as chips which held about three pounds in weight. The exotic mushrooms which are readily available today were still to make an appearance.

I used to cycle to the mushroom farm on the old trade bike. It had no gears and a pedal ratio of 1 to 1 so even a journey to Littlebourne was hard work.

Dad would buy four chips per week, two of button and two closed cap. This would be about Tuesday afternoon and by Saturday mornings they had all gone.

At Christmas and holidays times the order would double at least, and eventually they would be collected as part of the van delivery route. As with most small producers the supermarkets and wholesalers eventually took the market, the smaller producers couldn't keep up with the acres and acres of industrial sized mushroom sheds, finally it closed in the late 80s.

We didn't need to go far to get local produce, Mike Mayes at Treasury farm had a wholesale delivery lorry, George Holness, his driver went all over the area delivering potatoes to shops and outlets, in return he would pick up cabbages and cauliflowers for the regular customers, and pop them by on his way out in the morning.

Watercress was a luxury item but about a mile away in Wingham Well, was a small chalk stream which flowed over a gravel bed. This would enable this tasty salad item to be grown in abundance. This stream would meander down past Wingham, and out into the marshes where it would join the lesser Stour.

We would collect boxes and boxes of them in season from the Catt family and across the road Mr Davis owned a smallholding, he grew carrots, leeks, swedes, parsnips and purple sprouting broccoli. He employed a lovely guy, Herman.

Herman was of German descent and had been a prisoner of war in WW2. Being from a farming community he was used to tend the crops under supervision, but at the end of the war he elected to stay and eventually became part of the family, living in the house and working on the small holding.

He was probably one of the nicest men I have ever met. He was killed as a passenger in a tragic car crash and as a testament to his popularity, there was over two hundred mourners at his funeral.

The small holding on the Littlebourne road provided the soft fruit, apples pears and their speciality, gooseberries. This was owned by Mr Herbert Chapman (Herby). When he retired and sold the business, Herby came to work at the shop as the storeman, a job he had for many years.

In the shop cellar were several chest freezers with the overflow from the freezers in the shop sale area. The slabs of cheddar cheese were kept down there on shelves and the main safe was sitting proudly in the middle of the floor.

The safe must have been a couple of hundred years old, the key was similar to an old-fashioned gaoler's key from long ago! I always considered that key to be of the era of the stories of Toad, in the Wind in the Willows as he escaped from the town gaol after his driving misdemeanours.

In my lifetime there has been two floods where the pond overflowed and went down the street. The first time in 1969 it reached the garage entrance, but the second time in 1973 it went almost to the village green.

It was awful watching it run down the stairs into the cellar, the filthy brown coloured water was coming into the shop in an unstoppable torrent.

After a couple of hours, the freezers were bumping along the ceiling and eventually there was two feet of water in the shop, and three in the lower stores.

Neighbours, friends and family all came to help lift goods and all the boxes spread all over the lower store floor, packed the day before ready for the biggest delivery of the week, which just happened to be that day!

The fire brigade did come out with pumps and sandbags but by then the damage was done. Dad and mum together with my uncle Dennis, stayed up and worked nonstop for forty-eight hours, trying to arrange deliveries and supplies for the community.

The insurance company were very good, arranging a specialist firm to come in and remove the damaged stock and equipment. The whole process took weeks whilst they tried to work around the normal day to day activity, the smell of dank foul-smelling water permeated the shop.

The noise of a dozen de humidifiers rumbled twenty-four hours a day which vibrated and shook the Coombs brothers' side of the premises to complete distraction.

Once the shock of seeing the shop had sunk in it occurred to Dad that the garage further back along the road would also be under water. This unfortunately was equally problematic, the van and car had the water level with the door handles, and all you could see of my moped was the top of the mirrors.

My Uncle used his car for a few days to deliver groceries to the outlying areas until replacement vehicles could be sourced.

It took more than two years for things to return completely to normal, they always made a conscious effort to not put delivery boxes on the floors in the stores, pallets borrowed from the local farmers were used to give an airgap.

Perishables were displayed higher up in case of a repeat flood. Financially the were never compensated for the true cost, the loss adjuster was a little harsh and applied wear and tear to the fridges, display cabinets and freezers, and applied 'best guess' to some stock.

Through all of this trauma, it is worth noting that the elderly around the area still had their deliveries and goods, albeit late at night. Also, as an apology for being late and with some things missing, they had it given to them free of charge for the first couple of weeks after the disaster!

The most difficult organisation to deal with was the Post Office, it wouldn't let them close despite the safe containing all the money, stamps and postal orders, being under seven feet of water.

They sent out an emergency pack so pensions and stamps could be purchased, but collected it at close of play and stood over Dad whilst he did the end of day consolidation.

Dad was instructed to take the keys of the safe to the main office in Canterbury, and advise them when the water level reduced and exposed the safe.

Three people came from the main office and did an audit, just in case the whole thing was being staged to cover up fraudulent behaviours.

Dad never forgave them for that and was always wary of their intentions. The burglar alarm never worked properly again after the flood, the wiring must have been affected by the water as it was located on the stairs down into the cellar, it always had a problem in one way or another.

When it went off it woke the neighbours all around us and sometimes it did it two or three times a night. It didn't like cold weather, it had to be set for the insurance cover so it was a weekly routine wiping and cleaning all the electrical plates on the doors and windows to try and keep it functional.

As a teenager I used to take my turn and with a grumpy stance used to stomp off next door to reset the alarm. It never occurred to me that perhaps it was doing its job and we were actually being burgled!

The local farmers locally dug out the ditches and reinstated the drains, which over time, had become blocked by silt. The pond is the lowest collection point, the water runs downwards from Cherville gathering momentum as it goes.

A few years later the pond overflow was connected to the village drainage and thoroughly cleaned out, so removing the risk.

I recently found in my parents' paperwork a photograph of me walking down the pavement in the first flood when I was about eleven! A faded press cutting carefully cut out and stored.

My parents had a strong sense of community, realising the importance of serving the less mobile and isolated residents. They became aware of the growing use of the supermarkets, and knew they couldn't compete with the variety and pricing.

Everyone was becoming more mobile, cars sometimes two in every household was the norm, so a trip into town wasn't a day trip as it used to be with the bus.

Dad was involved with the Littlebourne and district branch of the Royal British Legion. He had been a member since 1948 when he left the services, he had held several branch offices during that time, including Chairman and President. I mention this as it links in with an annual event related to the villages.

Dad was also on the committee of the 'Ickham Charity' Every year he would arrange a grant from both organisations, and just before Christmas would bulk buy the old-fashioned tins of biscuits from Huntley and Palmers.

He would then wrap them in Christmas paper and hand deliver them personally around the area to the widows/widowers of the Legion members and to the widows/widowers living in the village.

The shop finally closed at the end of January 1991 after mum sustained a heart attack just before Christmas 1990. It was only some years later they told me they kept the shop open in the last three years at a huge loss, only surviving on the meagre salary the Post Office paid Dad for his efforts, as they knew some of the elderly community couldn't get their pensions and subsistence shopping, they needed to survive without their weekly delivery.

When they retired, they sold all their stock to other similar shops around the area. The bare shelves upstairs were pulled away revealing all the things that had fallen down the back over the years.

In one area the paper bags for putting fruit and veg into were piled in faded heaps. The bags had been stored in the same place since the beginning of time. Behind the shelves were thousands of them going back to the 1800s.

The next shelf was quite an odd shape. It was in a corner and when it was pulled out it revealed a small hidden alcove, going back nearly a metre. The treasure it revealed was amazing.

There were hundreds of loose 'ladies' products' going back through the ages. Quite an eye opener but I will leave this to the imagination, bottles of talcum powder and strange shaped empty bottles filled this hidden space.

Behind the next shelf were rolls of Izal and similar brands of toilet paper, covered in dust but still in good condition. Again, these went back to the 1940s, I can imagine what it was like to use them, they were like tracing paper but coarser, harping back to the carefully cut out newspapers from my early days in Bramling!

They finally handed back the keys and a lifetime of memories on the third of April, twenty years to the day of the start of the lease.

Two hundred years of the grocers' shop in Ickham was unceremoniously concluded with me climbing a ladder and prising the shop sign from the wall with a crowbar. It was so old it exploded when it hit the ground. Nothing remained it was now just a house.

The shop fittings were left in place after they left. Len Coombs had a desire to make the shop a rural life museum but his advancing years eventually beat him and the building stayed empty for about three years.

Len's nephew invited Dad to have a look around before the shop was cleared out ready for sale. In many ways he wished he hadn't gone, a lifetime of working memories was in that building, seeing it covered in thick green mould and dust really affected him.

The damp from the floods had still not gone and left untouched with no heating, had brought it all to the surface.

Fate dealt dad another blow, his father passed away in February and left him his little bungalow in Littlebourne. This was fortuitous as the lease of the shop came with Fern Cottage so eventually, they would have had to move from there.

In June 1991 they finally moved out of Ickham and settled into a happy retirement in Littlebourne, where they remained until they both passed away, mum in 2009 following a long decline through Alzheimer's disease, and dad through a rare condition, Guillain Barre syndrome which affects the central nervous system, in 2012.

Chapter six. Transition

I always wanted to be an engineer, it wasn't unusual as a small child to dismantle a bicycle newly gifted as a Christmas present, and reassemble it over a couple of days.

I always had a knack of repairing broken things and I thought it would be good to get some proper training, with a view to making it into a career.

My parents suggested that I follow them into the RAF and the prospect of repairing aeroplanes became attractive.

As I missed out on important parts of my education, I was always going down the route of a practical career using my hands and logic. It is only in recent times I have expanded my knowledge and effectively played 'catch up'.

As I couldn't join the RAF until I was seventeen, I spent the year after school working on the local farms and helping out in the shop. At sixteen I signed up for a moped licence.

One of my friends who went to Air Cadets with me had just passed his car test and gave me his moped. Again, I took it to pieces and rebuilt it and then started to see the local area under my own steam.

I had been in the Air Cadets since I was thirteen, and often went to RAF Manston to learn to fly gliders, and have experience flights in the Chipmunk two seat trainers. These were organised in rotation so we went down for the weekend and took advantage of the training.

For one reason or another, units who were booked in to attend sometimes just didn't turn up. This meant that the RAF staff were sitting around doing nothing for a weekend so, they used to offer the training to members of the local cadet units who were able to get there under their own steam.

We would add our names and phone numbers to a central list and I would sit near the telephone at 9am eagerly on a Saturday morning just in case it rang with good news. This happened frequently and I would spend hours flying around Kent in a chipmunk trainer learning to fly.

I was able to taxi, take off, fly unaided and finally land without any intervention by the pilot. Sometimes I would spend all weekend with the gliding school, again hours would be spent flying around the airfield perimeter. All thanks to having a moped!

Whilst holidaying in the USA over the years, I have been to a local flying school and hired a Cessna and an instructor and flew around the area, I flew over the Space Shuttle at Kennedy Space Centre before the events of 9/11.

When the time came to join up, passed the entrance test and attended the basic training in Lincolnshire. After ten days about half the intake was called in to be advised they had over recruited engineers and we were all to be transferred to either policemen or firemen.

I opted to leave and did an apprenticeship at the Casino garage somewhat nearer to home!

I followed a career through the motor trade eventually moving to the insurance industry as initially an assessor and then management and technical advisor, finally retiring in 2013. I spent twenty-seven years with the Territorial Army visiting places I would never have seen without that experience.

Photographs

White Cottage in Bramling as it is today, the wall along the front was complete and a small gate next to the house wall was the only access in 1962.

Myrtle Cottages opposite White Cottage (pulled down in the late 1960s) from a water colour by Fred Bennett. Maternal grandparents lived in the one furthest to the left.

Fred Bennett and Gladys Garrett on their first evening
out at the 'Casino ball room' in 1948.

ROADS FLOODED

Roads were flooded at Ickham after Friday's cloudburst. Here John Bennett picks his way home through the water.

Picture courtesy of the Gerry Warren, The KM Group.

The first flood in 1969 extended down as Fern Cottage, quite a surprise to wake up to in the morning! The photographer made me walk up and down the road for twenty minutes so he could get the shot he wanted!

The grocer in his shop, Fred Bennett worked there all his working life apart from his war service.

Wickhambreaux Mill, now luxury flats, note river bank earthed up, river diverted from its original course between Ickham and Wickhambreaux, to gain road access to and from the wheat milling production.

A zoom shot of what remains of the wood we used to camp in down the marshes to the rear of Seaton. It is sad to see the remaining trees are covered with ivy so their lifespan is coming to an end. In a few years there will be nothing left to see.

The school sign outside Wickhambreaux school with the building behind belonging to the Bower family completely unrecognisable now following building work.

The Duke William public house externally unchanged since the early 1950s

St John the Evangelist at Ickham, backdrop to many a game of cricket on the village green, and where my parents married in 1951.

Ickham high street from the north, unchanged over many years.

Wickhambreaux mill and the bridge over the Lesser Stour.

The Rose public house overlooking Wickhambreaux village green

Ickham post office and stores, photograph taken in 1973

St Andrews Church Wickhambreaux, standing guard on the village green since the thirteenth century.

The half-buried Pill box behind Ickham church where we played as children. It was sunken as during 1940 it was part of a defensive trench network which was ultimately filled in leaving it isolated.

Epilogue

As I conclude this book of childhood memories, I am struck by certain similarities to those early times. We are sitting here in 2020 in the midst of the Corona virus pandemic, not knowing what the outcome will look like, or indeed when!

A normal day would be a life full of busy people, driving everywhere, school runs, work, shopping and the general movement needed for recreation and the wealth of other things we do during our lives. Sitting here, I can hear birdsong, not only locally but the sound of skylarks in the fields, way beyond the paddock.

The sounds of pheasants and dogs barking way off in the distance albeit far away is audible where I know during what we call 'normal times' would never have been heard above the everyday hum.

This would not have been possible five weeks ago. The smell of the air, and I know this seems odd, but there is no pollution in the air we breathe now, in the country it smells just like I remember it all those years ago.

Aircraft movement would be always providing vapour trails high in the sky, crisscrossing in strange but comforting patterns. This with the lack of sound of multiple aircraft in the sky day and night. Today as I write, I haven't seen an aircraft at all.

I would conclude that with technology and as a more mobile population we have inadvertently given ourselves time to reflect on how we affect the planet around us and if we are careful, just maybe we will be so much more aware of how we need to look after it in the years to come.

We can never return to those simple times, but this pandemic has provided us a window on a world we inhabited long ago.

About the author

John Bennett was born in Canterbury and educated locally. In 1988 John left the motor trade and joined Sun Alliance insurance as a staff motor engineer where he progressed via a convoluted route to become a team leader of motor engineers in the North of England, Scotland and Northern Ireland.

John took early retirement in 2013 and is involved with the Princess of Wales's Royal Regiment (PWRR) Regimental association, assisting with its growth and development. John is also passionate about the Regimental Museum in Dover Castle and works as a volunteer assisting with outreach projects and doing talks and tours.

John is also on the Regimental heritage committee representing the TA and Army reserve. In addition, John is the Mental Health champion in the regimental association and is a qualified mental health first aider.

This is the fourth book John has written, the memoirs of his twenty-seven years serving the country, The Memories of a Rusty Cold War Warrior and Hell in my Head.

The latter is the story of three generations of my family who have suffered mental health problems as a result of conflict, and finally The Locked down Tiger who came to Tee, an irreverent look at a group of neighbours during lock down.

Acknowledgements

I would like to thank Michael and Clare Morpurgo for taking the time to engage with me and the marvellous foreword Michael has written at the beginning of the book. I would like to thank my wife Sue for the support and help given during the production of this book, the endless questions and common sense has been appreciated. Carol Kirk for the original suggestion and opinions on the book at various stages of writing. My old friends David Stevenson and Fiona Doherty for proof reading and common sense to ground me.
I would also like to thank my parents for leaving documents, photographs and diaries to help me with this book from the perspective of the shop in Ickham.

Steve Ray 1956 - 2021

Disclaimer

The writing contained within this book is based on my personal memories of events whilst growing up.
They may differ from the reality but they are remembered from the perspective of a child. I apologise in advance for errors and any upset caused. Any future reprints will correct any details deemed incorrect.

Printed in Great Britain
by Amazon

14736482R00066